Ronaldo

Andy Croft

Published in association with The Basic Skills Agency

Hodder & Stoughton

A MEMBER OF THE HODDER HEADLINE GROUP

Acknowledgements

Cover: Koji Aoki/AFLO/Getty Images

Photos: p. 4 © CONTIFOTO/CORBIS SYGMA; p. 9 © David Cannon/ALLSPORT; p. 13 © Matthew Ashton/EMPICS; p. 17 © Michael Steele/EMPICS; p. 24 © Action Press/Rex Features; p. 27 © PA Photos/EPA.

Orders: please contact Bookpoint Ltd, 130 Milton Park, Abingdon, Oxon OX14 4SB. Telephone (44) 01235 827720, Fax: (44) 01235 400454. Lines are open from 9.00–6.00, Monday to Saturday, with a 24 hour message answering service. You can also order through our website www.hoddereducation.co.uk

British Library Cataloguing in Publication Data
A catalogue record for this title is available from the British Library

ISBN 0 340 87651 4

First published 2003
Impression number   10 9 8 7 6 5 4 3 2
Year   2007 2206 2005 2004

Copyright © Andy Croft 2003

Typeset by SX Composing DTP, Rayleigh, Essex.
Printed in Great Britain for Hodder & Stoughton Educational, a division of Hodder Headline, 338 Euston Road, London NW1 3BH by Bath Press Ltd, Bath.

Contents

1 Fenomeno!

He scored in a World Cup final.
He won the Cup Winners' Cup.
He won the UEFA Cup.
In 1997, he was European Player of the Year.
In 2002, he won the World Cup Golden Boot.

He has been voted
World Footballer of the Year.
Three times!

He is the highest paid player
in the world.
He is the most expensive player
in the world.
He is the greatest player
in the world.

He is Ronaldo.

2 Beginnings

Ronaldo Luiz Nazario da Lima was born
on 22 September 1976.
He was born in Brazil.
He grew up
in a poor part of a big city.
It was called Rio de Janeiro.

His parents were called
Nelio and Sonia.
He was their third child.
His brother is called Nelinho
His sister is called Ione.

His parents split up
when he was 14.

Little Ronaldo had very curly hair.
His mother wanted him
to work hard at school.
But he just wanted
to play football.
Ronaldo didn't always go to school.
He preferred playing outside.
He played football on the streets.
Without any shoes on!
He thought the best player
was the Brazilian star Zico.

When Ronaldo was 11
he went for a trial.
It was with a famous club called Flamengo.
They turned him down.
Why?
Because he couldn't afford
the bus fare to the ground.

Little Ronaldo.

When he was 12
he joined a local indoor football team.
He started as a goalkeeper.
Soon he was playing as a striker.
He was strong in the air.
He was strong on the ground.
He had good close control.
He had pace.
He could shoot.
And he could score!

When he was 13
he joined an 11-a-side club called Sao Cristavao.
They were in the second division.
He scored 36 goals in 54 games for the club.
When he was 16
Cruzeiro bought him
for £30,000.
He scored 58 goals in 60 games for Cruzeiro.
He was the top scorer in the league.

3 Another Pele?

In 1993, Ronaldo played
for the Brazil under-17s team.
They played in the South American junior matches.
He scored 8 goals.

One year later he was in the Brazilian first team.
He was still only 17.
The great Pele was 17
when he first played for Brazil.

Ronaldo bought a car with his first wages.
Even though he wasn't old enough to drive!

Brazil's green and gold strip is famous.
Only the best players in the world can wear it.
Brazil have won the World Cup
more times than anyone else.
They are the best footballing country
in the world.

Ronaldo's first game for Brazil
was against Argentina.
Pele's first game
was also against Argentina.

Brazil already had a player called Ronaldo.
So the young Ronaldo was called Ronaldinho.
This means 'little Ronaldo'.

He scored his first goal for Brazil
against Iceland.
He was just 18.

He was in Brazil's World Cup squad in 1994.
He didn't play.
Brazil still won.
They were so good
they didn't need Ronaldo!
It was Brazil's fourth World Cup win.

Brazil's 1994 World Cup squad.

4 PSV Eindhoven

In 1994, Ronaldo moved to Holland.
PSV Eindhoven bought him.
For £4 million!

He was only 18 years old.
But no one could stop him scoring.
In two seasons, he scored 54 goals in 58 games.
In 1996, he was the top scorer in the Dutch league.
Ronaldo's curly hair and gap-toothed smile
were famous.

Then injury struck.
He hurt his right knee.
He went into hospital for an operation.
After the operation he trained very hard.
He was fit in time for the Dutch Cup Final.
But he only came on for a few minutes.
Ronaldo wasn't used to being on the bench.
He left PSV.

5 Barcelona

In 1997, Barcelona bought Ronaldo
for £13 million.
It was a world record.
He earned £2 million a year.

Ronaldo was now the most famous
player in the world.
He was playing for one
of the most famous clubs:
Barca.
He was playing at one
of the most famous grounds:
Nou Camp.

Ronaldo wore the No. 9 shirt.
Thousands of fans bought shirts
with his name on the back.
He shaved his head.
Fans copied him.
He wore a baseball cap.
Fans copied him.
When he scored he ran around
with his arms out,
like an aeroplane.
Fans copied him.

They called it Ronaldomania!

He scored in his first league game for Barca.
He scored 47 goals in 49 games.
That season, Barca were second
in the Spanish League.
They won the Spanish League Cup.
They won the European Cup Winners' Cup.
Ronaldo was the top scorer in the Spanish League
and in the Cup Winner's Cup.
He was also FIFA World Player of the Year.

Ronaldo scores for Barca in the UEFA Cup Winners Cup Final, 1997.

6 Inter Milan

Ronaldo wanted to stay with Barca.
But Inter Milan wanted to buy him.
In the summer of 1997
they bought him for £20 million.
It was another world record.

Ten thousand people waited to see him arrive.
Ten thousand people watched him start training.
The first time he played
for Inter Milan
there was a crowd of 50,000.

Some people said it was too much money.
He was still only 19.

But Ronaldo soon proved his critics wrong.
In his first season at Inter Milan,
he scored 34 goals in 47 games.
They came second in the league.
He helped Inter Milan win the UEFA Cup.
With another 6 goals.

The fans called him 'Fenomeno'.
Crowds followed him.
He started his own website.
Six million people tried to get online!

In his first season at Inter Milan
Ronaldo was the second highest scorer
in the Italian league.
He was the highest scorer in the UEFA Cup.
He was the highest scorer
in all European championships.
He was again voted FIFA World Player of the Year.
He beat Roberto Carlos,
Denis Bergkamp and Zinedine Zidane!

In five seasons,
Ronaldo scored 59 goals
in 99 games for Inter Milan.

Inter Milan's San Siro stadium.

7 World Cup 1998

In 1998, the World Cup was held in France.

People thought that Brazil would win again.

After all, they had Ronaldo.

The world's greatest striker.

So far, Ronaldo had scored 228 goals in 263 games.

He had scored 25 goals in 38 games for Brazil.

He was still only 21.

The World Cup started well.

Just as everyone expected.

Ronaldo scored against Morocco.

He scored twice against Chile.

He scored against Holland.

Brazil were in their sixth World Cup Final.

Just as everyone expected.

But on the day of the World Cup Final
Ronaldo became ill.
He was rushed away for tests.
The doctors couldn't find what was wrong.
Ronaldo decided to play.
He tried hard.
But everyone could see
there was a problem.
Without Ronaldo playing well, Brazil lost.
Nobody expected that.

But Ronaldo still came second
in FIFA's World Player ranking
(after Zidane).

8 Injuries

Ronaldo didn't want to talk
about the strange illness.
He just wanted to play for Inter Milan and Brazil.
At the start of the 1998 season
he scored 14 goals in 19 games.
He was top scorer
in the America's Cup with Brazil.
But his knee was hurting again.

Inter Milan had a new coach.
He was very hard on Ronaldo.
He made him train too much.
He left Ronaldo on the bench.

Then Ronaldo's right knee
stopped moving during a game.
He had to go back
for another operation.
Thousands of fans sat outside,
hoping to see their hero.
He was out for another four months.

Ronaldo was back in time for the Italian Cup Final,
against Lazio.
He started well.
Then a Lazio player kicked him from behind.
Six minutes into the game,
Ronaldo was through on goal.
The crowd held their breath.
Then disaster struck.
Ronaldo went down.
His right knee was broken.

Back in hospital,
crowds waited for him.
Ronaldo was in bed for a month.
He couldn't move.
Then he was on crutches.
Thousands of fans sent Get Well cards,
e-mails, faxes and even presents.
He went back to Brazil to get fit again.
Lots of famous people came to see him
and cheer him up.
Everybody said 'Volta!' ('Come back!').
There was a new Brazilian coach, Felipe Scolari.
He said the team could not play without him.

9 World Cup 2002

Ronaldo was out of football
for two and a half years.
But he was back in time for the World Cup
in Japan and South Korea.

Would his knee be strong enough?
Would he ever be as good again?
Could the greatest striker in the world
win the World Cup?

Ronaldo holding the World Cup for Brazil, 2002.

Ronaldo scored against Turkey.

He scored against China.

He scored twice against Costa Rica.

He scored against Belgium.

He scored against Turkey in the semi-final.

In the final he scored both goals
in Brazil's 2–0 defeat of Germany.

Brazil had won the World Cup for a record fifth time.

Ronaldo was voted man of the match.

He was the top scorer in the World Cup
with eight goals.

Ronaldo has now scored
45 goals in 69 games for Brazil.

10 Behind the Legend

Like most famous players
Ronaldo likes to be private.
He enjoys being at home.
He has a wife, Milene,
and a son, Ronald.

He enjoys playing tennis.
He likes the beach.
He doesn't drink.
His favourite food is pasta.

In September 2002,
Ronaldo joined Real Madrid.
The fee was £30 million.
He plays every week
at the Bernabau Stadium
in front of huge crowds.

Ronaldo with a group of handicapped chidren in Milan.

Ronaldo is very famous.
He is very rich.
But he has not forgotten where he came from.

He has set up a charity in Brazil.
For poor children.
He visits children in hospital.
He supports work on HIV and AIDS.
During the war in Kosovo
he went to the country.
He gave money to help rebuild a bombed school.
He and Zidane support the United Nations'
work against poverty and hunger.

Ronaldo once said,
'Every goal I score is a message
of hope for the poor'.